>>> **2002** • 11-year-old Courtney Joseph and 12-year-old Mary Leach look over their programs for "A Chorus Line."

ST. LOUIS POST-DISPATCH
BOOKS

ST. LOUIS POST-DISPATCH

THE MUNY

SONGS OF ST. LOUIS SUMMERS

BY
JUDITH
NEWMARK

Art director
Wade Wilson

Photo editor
Bill Keaggy

Assistant photo editor
Hillary Levin

Copy editor
Susan Hegger

Sales and marketing
Gail LaFata

Special thanks to Doug Weaver of Kansas City Star Books.
© 2007 St. Louis Post-Dispatch Books

ISBN 13: 978-0-9796054-0-6
ISNB 10: 0-9796054-0-7
Retail Price: $34.95

Printed by Walsworth Publishing Co., Marceline, Mo.

To order additional copies, call **1-800- 329-0224**
Order online at **www.post-dispatchstore.com**

1939: You can practically smell the face powder in this opening-night shot of chorus girls at their
dressing-room mirrors.

1968 • Children who play the Munchkins in "The Wizard of Oz" gather on the outdoor rehearsal stage to watch the leads in action.

CONTENTS

1948 • "One, two, rump, bump, bump!" cries Muny dance director Richard Barstow, teaching a combination to the chorus.

2005 • Rachel Cowin wears her Belle costume to see "Beauty and the Beast" at The Muny.

1948 • At a party for Muny entertainers at the Edward L. Kuhs estate in north St. Louis County, chorus girls play a "game of skill."

1940 • Dancers in "The American Way" keep busy knitting between rehearsal calls. They are (front row, from left) Virginia Conrad, Dolores Wein and Nancy McCabe; in the upper row (from left) are Iva Lee Cook, Helen Rosler, Mary Louise Crowe, Ruth Katt and Jane Fox.

INTRODUCTION

The story of The Muny, the enormous outdoor theater in Forest Park, darts through the history of St. Louis like a dance and resonates like a song.

The Muny is the first theater generations of St. Louisans have attended — and it's the one that, consciously or not, they'll judge all others against.

That's a heck of a reputation to live up to.

Imposing in its size (the largest outdoor theater in America) and extravagant in its ambition (the cultural enrichment of a community), The Muny has always specialized in musical theater. Song and dance are its stock in trade; the civilized and civilizing pleasures of musical summer nights are its signal, sustained achievement.

The Muny planted roots in the park before World War I. Probably inspired by the success of an enormous 1914 civic pageant on Art Hill, community leaders decided in 1916 to mark the 300th anniversary of William Shakespeare's death with a production of "As You Like It."

The play starred Margaret Anglin, a famous Broadway actress who headed her own company. (It included two young actors destined for great things: Sidney Greenstreet, who played Touchstone here, and Alfred Lunt, who took several small roles.) But Anglin chose not to perform on Art Hill.

According to legend, she walked around Forest Park until she came to the present Muny site. Perhaps channeling the gods of theater, perhaps inspired by canny hints from civil

engineers, Margaret Anglin is said to have raised her arms and pointed to the perfect spot for her production, right between two tall oak trees.

That place would evolve into The Muny, and it wouldn't take long to happen.

The very next year, 1917, the St. Louis Advertising Club sponsored a production of Verdi's opera "Aida" there, building a crude theater on Anglin's designated spot. In 1918, as World War I drew to its desperately welcomed close, St. Louis Mayor Henry Kiel led an effort to improve the site.

He and his colleagues envisioned a permanent theater with a real season. The Municipal Theatre Association, parent of The Muny, was incorporated on June 10, 1919. Six days later, it opened its first show, "Robin Hood." Kiel appeared in the show himself, playing King Richard.

Thousands of people saw "Robin Hood." Millions more have been to The Muny since then, coming together night after summer night for no reason except to enjoy songs and dances together. They go to a city park and sit among strangers; they leave after dark unintimidated, whistling their favorite tunes and comparing the show they just saw to other productions. They return for something else next week.

Most of these people go to The Muny without a thought for Henry Kiel and whatever community dreams he may have treasured. They don't need to think about that. They live it, instead.

They are the audience a long-ago mayor imagined.

They — we — are St. Louis, and The Muny is one of the few places where we get the chance to appreciate precisely how much that means.

<<< **2002** • "A Chorus Line," a show about young dancers, naturally opens with a dance audition.

1967 • Bob Holiday, star of "It's a Bird . . . It's a Plane . . . It's Superman," stands high above his fellow performers (from left) Richard France, Karen Morrow, Charles Nelson Reilly and Gary Oakes.

>>> 2006 • Jeb Brown, as Zoser, plots evil-doings in "Aida."

THE SCOPE

A favorite St. Louis urban legend isn't true. No Broadway star ever stepped onto The Muny stage, looked out at the size of the house and fainted.

But everybody who believed it had good reason.

In terms of size, there isn't much to rival The Muny, the biggest outdoor theater in the United States and one of the biggest anywhere. Even its statistics boggle the imagination.

The Muny seats an audience of 10,779. Looking for a comparison? A typical Broadway theater seats about 1,200.

When The Muny stages a popular show like "The Wizard of Oz," it employs a full chorus of about 30 adults, plus about 100 children. They do not crowd the stage.

That "working" stage is 90 feet deep and 110 feet wide. For comparison, consider New York's Majestic Theatre, where "The Phantom of the Opera" began its phenomenal run in 1988. The Majestic stage is 40 feet, 10 inches deep and 47 feet, 10 inches wide. It's considered a large Broadway house.

When the stage is used at its maximum size, as it was for "Miss Saigon," it's about half the size of a football field. Methods of transportation over and across it have included horses, an elephant, fancy cars, hot air balloons and a helicopter. None involved special effects.

1963 • An aerial view of The Muny extends from the upper parking lot (at left) through the seats and the stage to the backstage area (at right). In all, the theater covers more than 6 acres.

The theater, overall, has a footprint of over six acres in Forest Park. It adds up to an extravagant notion of theater, outsized and out of this world.

1920 • From the start, The Muny draws — and accommodates — big crowds.

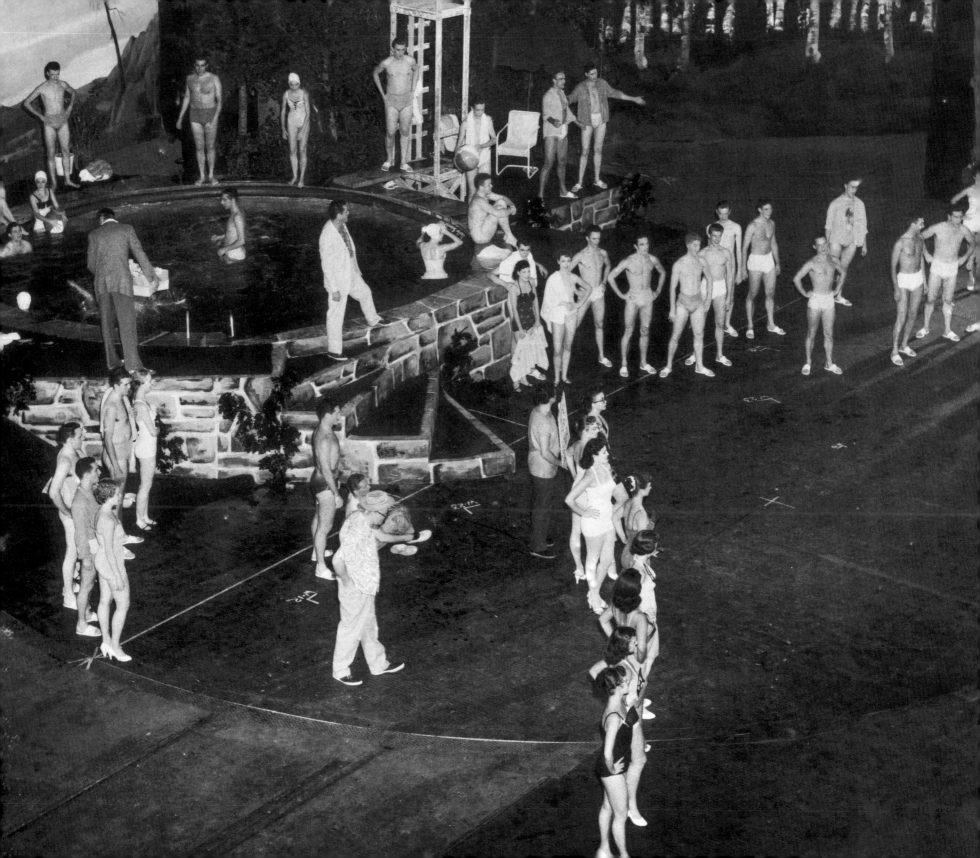

<<< **1956** • A real swimming pool dominates The Muny stage in "Wish You Were Here." Made of reinforced plastic, the pool was 22 feet in diameter and more than 3 feet deep.

>>> **1962** • Pierre Olaf (left) and Cyril Ritchard soar over The Muny stage in "Around the World in 80 Days." An 80-foot crane lifted their balloon, a good example of the open-air theater's unusual flexibility. The Muny staged another aviation coup in 2001, when a real helicopter arrived for the dramatic evacuation scene in "Miss Saigon."

>>> **1928** • It takes a lot of entertainers to fill The Muny stage. When the army of Ruritania parades in "Princess Flavia," it makes an impressive show, complete with coed troops.

19

<<< 1974 • Stage hands set up scaffolding for "Mack and Mabel." To appreciate the scale of the set, compare the height of the men and their ladder to the structure that towers above them.

>>> 1951 • Ben F. Lamb (left), the head of the weigher's office at St. Louis's main post office on Market Street, accepts more than 20 sacks of season tickets from The Muny's box office manager, Cecil Cronkhite. The shipment to subscribers was worth close to $340,000.

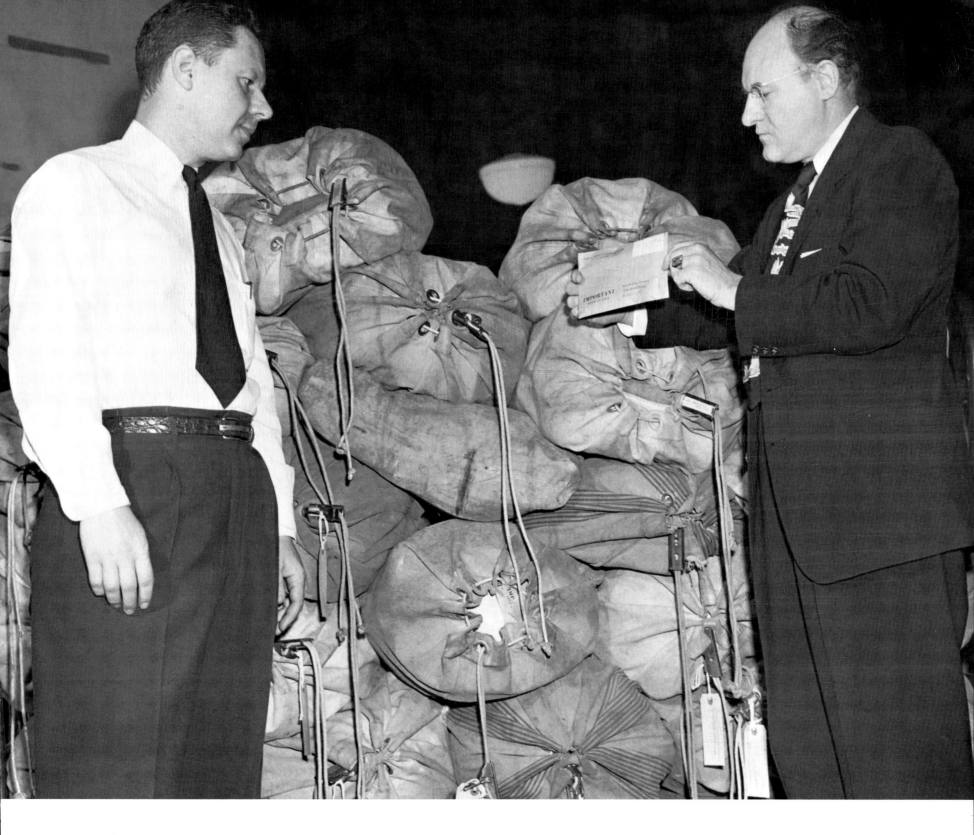

1943 • A panoramic photo made from three separate images captures The Muny on July 17, the night that a record-breaking audience of 11,407 people turned out for "The Great Waltz." It's the largest crowd in Muny history. The show went on to break weekly attendance records, drawing 78,138 theater-goers over seven nights.

<<< **2003** •
Trees in full leaf reveal The Muny as one of the greenest theaters in the world, from its upper pavilion (at the bottom of the photo) through the stage, the seats and the lower parking lot.

THE STARS

Ethel Merman and Zero Mostel, Lauren Bacall and Yul Brynner, Pearl Bailey and Joel Grey — those are marquee names. Neon names. Broadway names.

They're Muny names as well.

Plenty of stars played The Muny at the height of their careers. It's a long list. Over the years, others twinkling in the constellation have included Gene Kelly, W.C. Fields, Carol Burnett, Rock Hudson, Sid Caesar, Lynn Redgrave, John Raitt, Elaine Stritch and Soupy Sales. Olympic gymnast Cathy Rigby made her Muny debut as Peter Pan; football great Joe Namath, flirting with a stage career, starred in "Li'l Abner."

Star names were especially ample in the 1970s. At that time, The Muny presented many national tours of recent Broadway hits, often featuring the original stars.

The sets, however, didn't fit the big stage, and The Muny season was at the mercy of multi-city tour schedules. When Paul Blake became executive producer in 1990, he returned the outdoor theater to its roots, staging virtually every show at The Muny and for The Muny. Observing that there are many more talented performers than famous ones, Blake shifted the emphasis from big names and put it on big shows instead.

Under Blake's system, plenty of important artists still play The Muny. Others blossom there. Ashley Brown, a Muny ingenue, went on to open in the title role of "Mary Poppins" on Broadway. Ken Page got his start in the Muny chorus, then created the role of "Old Deuteronomy" in "Cats" — a signature role he reprised at The Muny.

In a way, that's an old tradition that's come back. Young performers who appeared at The Muny early in their careers include Betty Grable, Irene Dunne, Virginia Mayo and Red Skelton. If you search the old programs, you might even find a stock baritone named Archibald Leach. But you probably know him better as Cary Grant.

1984 • Ann Miller and Mickey Rooney bring back burlesque in "Sugar Babies."

1938 • Richard Skelton (third from the right), later known as Red, plays a West Point cadet in a Civil War operetta, "Gentlemen Unafraid."

1974 • Gene Kelly, one of the greatest dancers in American entertainment history, does an old-fashioned soft shoe as Sid in "Take Me Along."

<<< **1969** • Choreographer Tommy Tune rehearses a "State Fair" number with Bonnie Schon. Tune also appeared in the world-premiere stage musical, which starred Ozzie and Harriet Nelson.

>>> **1981** • Robert Goulet comes "to wive it wealthily in Padua" as the star of Cole Porter's "Kiss Me, Kate."

<<< 1993 • Olympic gymnast Cathy Rigby stars in "Annie Get Your Gun" with Mauricio Bustamante. Muny audiences knew her high-flying turns in "Peter Pan," too.

>>> 1997 • Bob Keeshan, TV's beloved Captain Kangaroo, takes a break at rehearsal for "The Wizard of Oz" with his granddaughter, Kaelan Sullivan. She was one of 100 St. Louis children in the production; Keeshan played the Wizard.

>>> 1957 • Juanita Hall, who won a Tony Award and much acclaim when she played Bloody Mary in the original Broadway production of "South Pacific," reprises the role at The Muny. Another musical theater veteran, Benny Baker, plays a Seabee.

<<< **1968** • Douglas Fairbanks Jr. stars in "My Fair Lady" as phonetics authority Henry Higgins. He'll make a lady of the Cockney flower girl Eliza, played by Margot Moser.

<<< 1970 • Tony-winner Joel Grey plays the title role in "George M!," a biography of legendary showman George M. Cohan. The cast also includes (from left) Patti Mariano, Betty Ann Grove and Richard France.

>>> 1977 • Richard Roundtree plays the smooth gambler Sky Masterson and Leslie Uggams is the "mission doll" out to reform him in "Guys and Dolls."

1976 • Zero Mostel recreates his signature role, Tevye the dairyman, when "Fiddler on the Roof" plays The Muny.

>>> 1931 • Director Lew Morton (seated, holding a script) starts rehearsal for a new show with his cast. Notice the tall man standing fifth from the left, a minor player here. But movie stardom was just around the corner for Archie Leach, soon to change his name to Cary Grant.

>>> **1958** • Bob Hope rehearses for "Roberta" on the open-air platform.

40

1977 • A chorus of enthusiastic Brazilian sailors carry away Lauren Bacall, conga-style, in "Wonderful Town."

<<< **1968** • Ethel Merman, the musical comedy star whose big, belting voice defined shows from "Anything Goes" to "Gypsy," plays an ambassador in "Call Me Madam." The cast included Richard Eastham (left) and Russell Nype.

>>> **1975** • Ed Ames (right) relaxes backstage with Patti Davis and Robert Darnell, his costars in "Carousel." Ames plays Billy Bigelow, a good-hearted, quick-tempered roustabout whose "Soliloquy" to his unborn child is a showpiece for baritones and a favorite with dads.

<<< 1966 • Broadway dance star Gretchen Wyler rehearses "Bye Bye Birdie" with Dick Patterson. She got her start in The Muny chorus in 1950, then announced her retirement from show business when she played the title role in "Hello, Dolly!" at The Muny in 1997. In between, Muny audiences enjoyed her performances in a number of roles.

>>> 1968 • Co-stars Jaye P. Morgan and John Raitt chuckle over the script to "The Pajama Game."

<<< 1973 • Debbie Reynolds, a favorite with Muny audiences, stars in a revival of "Irene" with Monte Markham.

>>> 1971 • Pearl Bailey and Cab Calloway bring their Broadway triumph, "Hello, Dolly!," to The Muny stage.

THE CHORUS

The Muny chorus, training ground for generations of young performers, has been known almost since the beginning for several things:
- Great experience.
- Incredibly hard work.
- A credit that adds a decidedly professional cachet to a young performer's resume.

Year after year, hundreds of aspiring singers and dancers have tried out for The Muny chorus, a challenging audition. At one time, nearly all the chorus members came from the St. Louis area; today, they come from throughout the Midwest, and even farther.

They hope to be chosen for a distinguished line whose alumni include Betty Grable, Irene Dunne, Virginia Mayo, Virginia Gibson, Ken Page and Ashley Brown.

Up until the mid-1970s, members of the chorus were hired for the whole season. It was a grueling schedule, with week after week of performing in one show at night and rehearsing another in the daytime.

In recent years, most chorus members are hired for only a few shows during the season. It's still pretty tough, though, especially because the shows go up in only 11 days. Most of the chorus members had more time rehearsing for their high school musicals (which nearly all of them were in).

They rehearse in the daytime, when it's hot, and perform at night, when it's also hot. They may be asked to crawl around the stage in wolf costumes, to sing lustily while balancing platters of food or to dress for winter in Russia during August in St. Louis.

And they seem to love it. Thanks to the chorus, more performers have earned their membership in Actors Equity at The Muny than anywhere else in the Midwest.

1934 • Muny chorus girls rehearse at the American Theatre downtown, getting a headstart on the summer season. They are (from left) Lala Bauman (who would go on to teach many St. Louis dancers), Peggy Phillips, Sally Argo and Rosemary Powell.

1942 • For many years Muny chorus members worked the entire season, not just one or two shows. That meant they started rehearsals before the first show opened, then performed at night and rehearsed their next show during the day. It was a tough schedule, but performers competed hard to make the cut. Most of the 1942 female dancers were from the St. Louis area. From left, by row, they are: (first row) Mary Ann Hickey, Susan Scott, Eunice Kagan, Jean Haumueller, (second row) Rosemary Powell, Leonore Hines, Jane Bauer, Carol Ossman, (third row) Doris Jean Rathman, Virginia Hashagen, Lillian Cross, Virginia Conrad, (fourth row) Lillian Ann Merod, Virginia Lee Green, Marie von Behren, Betty Herbert, (fifth row) Nancy McCabe, Jackie Bonder, Kay Eibert, Suzanne Schmitz, (last row) Mary Foster, Josephine McCann, Dortha Maie Wicker and Mary Jo Zucchero.

1969 • Resident choreographer Jack Beaber (far left) studies four dancers who hope to earn a spot in the Muny chorus.

<<< 1948 • Wardrobe mistress Clara Laubersheimer fits Virginia Gorski (standing on table), a new member of The Muny chorus, for her costume. She went on to Hollywood fame as Virginia Gibson, one of the stars of "Seven Brides for Seven Brothers." The other dancers being fitted are Jeanne Griffin (foreground) and Bernetta Hart.

1959 • "The King and I" demands a special chorus to play the Siamese ruler's many children. Production director John Kennedy gives tips to some of the girls who've been cast: (from left) Kimi Nanoe, Joyce Hayashi, Lynn Shimamoto, Peggy Ann Ikeda, Valerie Jane Ikeda, Debbie Hong, Elaine Uchiyama, Donna Marie Cope, Lois Shimamoto and Naomi Takemoto.

1942 • The men's vocal chorus warms up for a season that includes "Show Boat," "Roberta" and "The Wizard of Oz." The performers are, from left (front row) Bob Herman, Kenneth Cantrill, Bill Thompson, Fred Schneider, Everett Young, Lyndon Crews, (second row) Randles Watkins, Vernon Gutjahr, Wilbert Liebling, George Irving, James Stanley, George Mueller and Eden Nichols.

1977 • Bill Perinis warms up for auditions with a good upside-down stretch.

<<< 1934 • The large "Show Boat" ensemble gathers on The Muny stage before dress rehearsal. The cast is racially integrated – unusual for its day but vital to the show. Written by Jerome Kern and Oscar Hammerstein II, it's the most popular show in Muny history, with 14 productions between 1930 and the latest one, in 2003.

1939 • The east platform has been revamped, but rehearsals still take place there – in the daytime, in the heat, sometimes in the rain. Performers – like these chorus members rehearsing for "Katinka" – look at it as part of The Muny experience. In 2007, a new 2-story rehearsal hall opened – with air conditioning.

>>> 1973 • Scaffolds that will support scenery in "South Pacific" turn into a kind of jungle-gym for members of the dance chorus. The dancer in the middle of the top row, Mark Krupinski, will go on to direct the Muny Kids and Muny Teens. From left, the dancers are (top row) Don Coven, Krupinski, Mike Michael, (center row) Jim Kolb, Barbara Bangert, Mark Trares, (front row) Sharon Halley, Mary Beth Kisner, Mimi Schechter, Timothy Schnell, Carol Basch and Millie Garvey.

1965 • As the trolley goes clang, clang, clang, members of the chorus back up star Anita Gillette in the quintessential Muny show, "Meet Me in St. Louis." The old-fashioned coats and hats may not be ideal for a summer night in St. Louis. But the chorus' outfits help set the mood for every production, so costumes must be colorful and period-perfect.

1993 • Waiting to audition, Karen Klaskin fills out her resume on the lawn outside the theater.

2006 • Skirts swirl and boys lift girls to create a classic Muny chorus moment in "Seven Brides for Seven Brothers." The big chorus is famed for this kind of staging, which plays beautifully at the big outdoor theater.

1993 • Sister Melinda Fischer (left), a school principal in Alton, pauses backstage to look over a program with Shirley Long (center) and Sherry Smith, who are just playing nuns at The Muny. All three sing in the convent chorus in "The Sound of Music."

<<< 1947 • After their opening-night bows, members of the chorus of "The Dancing Years" return to the dressing rooms. The show ran 10 more nights.

1965 • Chorus members ride "horses" for the jousting scene in "Camelot." Or to look at it a little differently, they wear horses, which fit around them with big panels, like a Martha Washington dress.

1982 • Joan Oberndorf stretches and hydrates as she waits for her turn to try out for The Muny.

<<< **1946** • Stars in "The Wizard of Oz" – Robert E. Perry as the Tin Woodman, Eric Brotherson as the Scarecrow and Edmund Dorsay as the Cowardly Lion – chat with members of the children's chorus during intermission. The girls are (from left) Donna Muffler, Marcia Mae Koslow, Jackie Mrsich, Carol Kaimann and Joan Love.

>>> **1950** • During auditions, dance director John Butler teaches a routine to Jane Bergmeier (foreground) and other aspiring members of the chorus.

<<< **1945** • Chorus members like Jean Bantle (foreground) and Norma Steinmetz (right) get used to sharing crowded dressing rooms.

>>> **1943** • Lunchtime! Members of the chorus are ready for a break.

AT REHEARSAL

It's a killer schedule.

Muny shows go up in 11 days. These are full-scale, full-length musical productions — shows that most theaters would take four to six weeks to stage. If the show is to open on Broadway, rehearsal can last months.

But at The Muny, there's really no alternative. Each show has to be ready to open as soon as its predecessor closes. That means the performers and members of the crew have to work hard, work fast and be ready to turn on a dime.

There's no room for slack. Principals show up for the first rehearsal knowing their lines and their music. Chorus dancers must be able to learn a combination in the morning and perform it in the afternoon. Members of the orchestra turn to familiar shows with pleasure and learn new scores in a hurry. (How can you tell a Muny score sheet? By the dead bugs squashed on the pages.)

Muny shows open on Monday nights. That means the set for the preceding show is onstage until about 20 hours before opening.

To pull it all together, there's a special rehearsal early Sunday morning. It starts at midnight, after the Saturday-night crowd is gone, and lasts until 5 a.m. That's the only tech rehearsal (with lights and sound), before the opening. Thanks to an energetic, disciplined crew, the other show's set goes back in place before its final performance on Sunday night.

Working with that kind of pressure takes imagination and stamina. But by 8:15 p.m. on Monday, the audience should think that it looks easy. They usually do.

1953 • Morton DaCosta (center) cues Lawrence Brooks, who's playing the title role in the world-premiere musical "Rip Van Winkle." DaCosta wrote the book and lyrics for the show, which he also directs; Edwin McArthur, The Muny's musical director, is the composer.

1945 • Gil Johnson and Jane Johnson rehearse a lively number for "Jubilee," the opening show of the 1945 season.

>>> **1959** • As Alice Nunn listens in the wings for her cue, Hans Conreid continues to study his "Song of Norway" script. It's dress rehearsal. The rapid production pace at The Muny makes every moment count.

<<< **1920** • Rehearsals for The Muny's productions take place during the day. This cast will perform "The Mikado."

1973 • Michele Lee asks her director a question during rehearsal for "Seesaw." This production moved to The Muny from Broadway – cast, props and all.

>>> **1999** •
Playing Martha
Jefferson in "1776,"
Andrea Burns
practices a song in
her dressing room.

1947 • Singers, dancers, actors and musicians grab a bite during a break in their all-night dress rehearsal.

<<< **1959** • Muny production manager John Kennedy watches performers rehearse on the outdoor platform. The other directors' chairs are reserved for music director Edwin McArthur and director Edward M. Greenberg.

>>> **1939** • Nancy McCord rehearses her elopement scene in "Katinka." No doubt onstage she'll wear more forgiving shoes.

<<< **1944** • Comedians Zamah Cunningham and Billy Lynn go over their lines.

>>> **1941** • As The Muny prepares for the world premiere of a show called "New Orleans," rehearsals for the untried vehicle often last until dawn. No wonder dancer Lucille Cartier and Muny office worker Donald Dunham need to grab a quick nap.

BEHIND THE SCENES

Not everybody who works at The Muny takes curtain calls.

But without them, the show doesn't go on.

All theatrical performances entail a variety of backstage crafts, such as wardrobe, set design and construction, painting, lighting and sound. Ticket-sellers, ushers, vendors and guards are also essential to The Muny. In all, about 700 men and women work at the theater every summer.

And they work hard. At The Muny, where shows typically go from start to opening night in under two weeks, everybody from stagehand to star has to work at a breakneck pace.

Yet many of the workers return year after year. Once they get into the rhythm, their jobs offer a particular satisfaction: quick results.

And on the very last night of the season, there are curtain calls for all. The entire crew joins the performers onstage to sing "Auld Lang Syne" with the audience — already looking forward to the season ahead.

1917 • Workers building The Muny haul away dirt and debris in carts drawn by horses and mules. The photographer taking this shot stood where the stage would soon rise.

1938 • Seamstresses put finishing touches on elaborate costumes for "Virginia." The costumes were so valuable - $60,000! - that two park police officers, Sgt. William Hilsman (left) and Peter J. Rammacher, were on duty to protect the women and their wares.

>>> 1959 • Chorus singers (from left) Barbara Stevens, Lynette Bennett and Cheri Ann Schear stroll backstage with some of their fellow "performers." The animals – a goose, two pigs and a beagle – appeared in a barnyard scene in "Li'l Abner." Animal trainers and wranglers are on hand whenever their performers are.

2004 • Cement mason Doug Hampton restores the cupola atop The Muny.

<<< **1930** • Workmen install a revolving turntable, a modern stage device that dramatically shortens the time it takes to change scenes. It's 48 feet in diameter, the largest outdoor turntable in the United States. Now computerized, it still works.

>>> **1967** • Jim Saunders, an expert in on-stage flying, doublechecks the equipment that allows the hero of "It's a Bird . . . It's a Plane . . . It's Superman" to be mistaken for birds and planes.

<<< **1949** • A painter freshens up the seats, electricians check the footlights and carpenters climb the scaffolds on the stage as the dance chorus gets ready to open in "Balalaika."

>>> **1946** • Stagehands with squeegees mop up after a rainstorm. The show must go on — but until the stage is safely dry, the dancers can't.

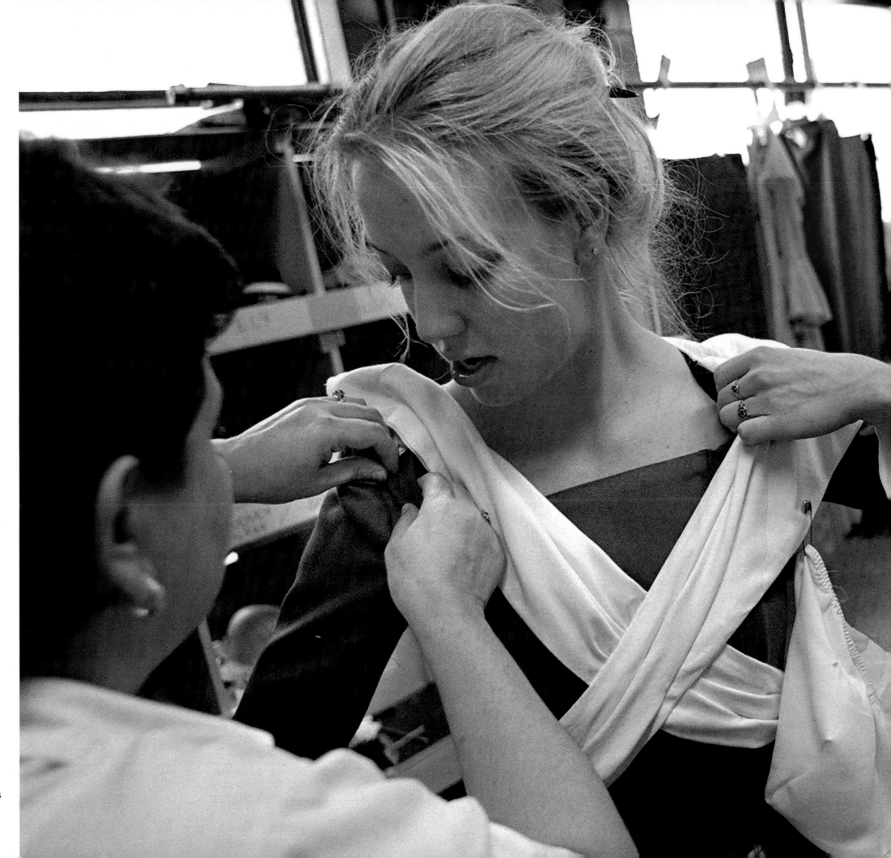

1935 • Tree surgeons cut decayed spots from the huge oaks that frame The Muny stage left and right. In 2002, when the tree at stage right could no longer be saved, it was cut down for safety reasons and made into a big table, the centerpiece of The Muny conference room.

<<< 2001 • Wardrobe mistress Gina Mackinnon fits Sarah Engelke in her "Brigadoon" costume. Two other members of the chorus, Melissa Gietzen and Jessica Holzem, stand ready for their fittings, too.

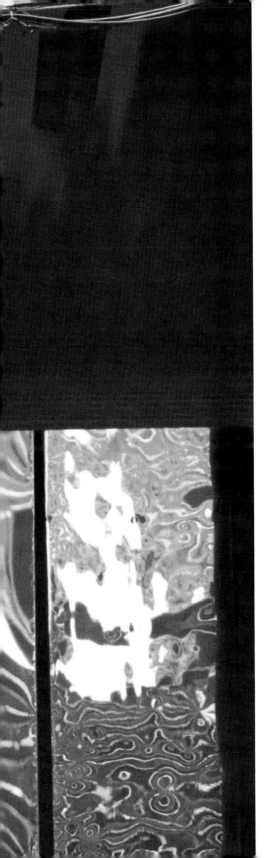

>>> 2001 • Set painter Cara Haley puts finishing touches on a big Celtic cross, part of the "Brigadoon" set.

<<< 1989 • Tim McDonald spray-paints the underside of a baffle on the set of "A Chorus Line."

91

<<< **1942** • Sound operators Maurice Hurley (kneeling) and Ben Bender (standing, right) install new sound control panels, with advice from William F. Uphouse of Southwestern Bell Telephone Co.

>>> **1938** • Box office staffers (from left) Ann Woodward, Leona Hines, Cecil Cronkhite and Nat Hall have their hands full. More than 800,000 tickets had to be sorted – manually – before the season opens.

1939 • Art director Norris Houghton sketches ideas for a set. He works about three weeks in advance.

<<< 1980 • It's January, but master stage carpenter Jim Murphy is back at The Muny, looking over stage sets and props. Many pieces can be refurbished for use season after season.

<<< **2001** • As stagehand Greg Stone constructs a set for the annual children's show, he gradually seems to be working in the Land of Oz.

97

<<< **1944** • In the dark, stagehands move scenery between acts.

>>> **1954** • Propmaster Frank Allen touches up a figurine, one of the many items in his storehouse. You never know what the next play will call for.

1978 • Three different dogs play Sandy in "Annie" at The Muny. In real life their handler, Jeanne Hand, and their owner-trainer, Leonard Brook, know them as (from left) Boy, Ruth and Zack.

1940 • O.J. Vanasse, assistant stage director of "The American Way," gives opening-night instructions to young St. Louisans who appear in the big show. They are (front row, from left) Sidney Cohen, Joseph Maley, Jackie Herman, Rosalie Appt, Wayne Wachter, Joe Guccione and Neal Oxenhandler; behind them (from left) are Rolland Bierach, Charles Bartman, Barry Mineah, Dick Wachter, Billie Lou Watt, Mary Sue Curry, Patricia Mae Curry, Allan Gordon and Gene Adams.

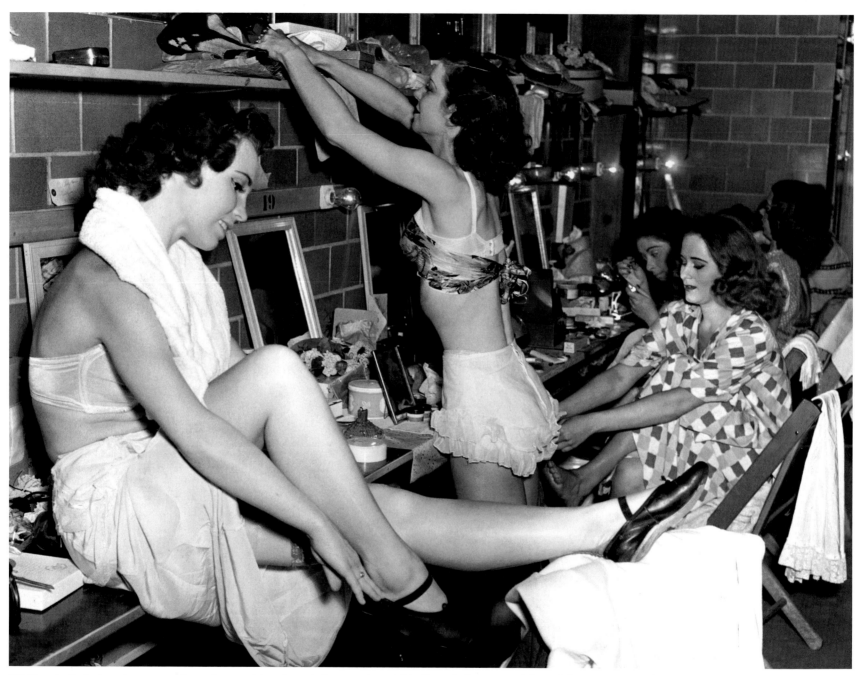

1950 • In their dressing room, Muny chorus girls get ready for opening night. Those in foreground (from left) are Joan Padfield, Bunny Foster and Gretchen Wienecke, who later stars at The Muny and on Broadway under a more glamorous name: Gretchen Wyler.

1975 • As season tickets go on sale, Muny staffers Ed Bowdern (center, holding a "Wednesday" seating chart) and Jim Devous help patrons choose their seats.

THE MUSIC

Rodgers and Hammerstein, Irving Berlin, Lerner and Loewe, Cole Porter, Boublil and Schonberg, Steven Sondheim, Gilbert and Sullivan, Frank Loesser: Name your favorite musical theater creators, and there's a good chance that you heard their work at The Muny.

Lucky you. If you heard it there, you heard it the way you should have.

The Muny has always used a big, Broadway-sized orchestra. It didn't have to. A lot of theaters use rescored treatments for small ensembles, sometimes boosted with synthesized enhancements. They can sound good.

But that isn't The Muny way. Even as big, human orchestras have come to seem like a dated luxury in some quarters, The Muny has continued to perform shows with that kind of ensemble, relishing its color and its volume. That has persisted even in a technically enhanced world that minimizes distinctions among a small combo, a synthesizer and a veteran 30-man orchestra in the pit

You know who could tell? Richard Rodgers, Irving Berlin, Frederick Loewe, Cole Porter — and, whether they know it or not, many of their fans. The traditional, well-trained orchestra pit at The Muny strives to express the bold Broadway sound so vibrantly that it could satisfy the composers who defined it in the first place.

1969 • At The Muny, composer Richard Rodgers is a kind of god. The shows he created with lyricist Oscar Hammerstein III — "South Pacific," "The Sound of Music," "Oklahoma!" and more — go a long way toward defining the Golden Age of American musical theater, and The Muny's sound. Here for a performance of his show "State Fair," Rodgers treated fans to a short piano concert.

1937 • Vocalists audition for The Muny chorus.

<<< **1968** • Violinist Charlene Clark and other members of the orchestra rehearse for "The Sound of Music."

>>> **1916** • The Muny, still under construction, offers wooden folding chairs to the audience and a spot to the side of the natural stage to the musicians. "As You Like It," of course, normally does not include an orchestra. It's almost as if the site demanded one from the start.

1939 • Prior to Monday's opening-night show, the orchestra and performers rehearse together for the first, and only, time on Sunday afternoon. To protect themselves from the sun, many musicians don pith helmets, straw boaters or other hats.

<<< 1948 • Margaret Ann Bensiek auditions for The Muny's production of "Sari," a show with a children's violin section. Muny music director Edwin McArthur (left) and other judges listen closely to the 7-year-old girl.

>>> **2002** • Jerry Bolen, a longtime Muny percussionist, rehearses for "A Chorus Line."

2006 • Music director Kevin Farrell leads the orchestra in rehearsal for "The King and I."

<<< 1934 • In May, The Muny's musicians and singing chorus perform a concert that features selections from the coming season. An enormous audience comes for a taste of the season ahead.

>>> 1981 • The St. Louis Symphony Orchestra settles into The Muny pit to rehearse for "A Grand Night for Singing," a revue featuring performers from Opera Theatre of St. Louis.

SPECIAL TWISTS

The first show at what we now call The Muny wasn't a musical at all. It was "As You Like It," a title that makes the Shakespeare Festival of St. Louis, which also performs in Forest Park, a sort of metaphorical Muny offshoot.

Things changed quickly, however, and musicals have dominated the big outdoor theater for nearly its entire history.

But The Muny has been home to all kinds of entertainment: children's pageants, war bond rallies and a yodeling contest, as well as dance concerts folkloric and classical. Over the years, The Muny stage has often been favored with pop concerts by stars, including laid-back James Taylor, suave Burt Bacharach, the kookie duet Sonny and Cher, and the New Wave's B-52s. When a popular novelty act was available, it was no big deal to tuck it right into a show.

Among the most elegant performances had to be the fashion extravaganzas of the 1920s. All the big Washington Avenue clothing manufacturers took part. Whether or not you could afford to shop at the best stores, at The Muny everyone could cast an appraising eye on suits from Rice-Stix, evening ensembles from Ely & Walker, furs from Landers and Pearlman, footwear from Brown Shoe, jewelry from C.R. Hettel and much more.

1942 • Katherine Salkey (left) of the American Women's Voluntary Services and Margaret Stinson (right) of The Muny chorus sell a war stamp corsage to a member of the audience, Catherine Bazdarich (center). The evening is a triumph, raising $35,000 for the war effort and $9,600 for the Army and Navy Relief Funds.

1942 • In the summer, children from parks around St. Louis present playground pageants at The Muny. About 1,600 children from 33 playgrounds contribute scenes to a production of "Cinderella." They perform their show during the daytime.

<<< **1939** • Big dance numbers that create a visual panorama become a Muny staple. "On Your Toes" offers loads of opportunities with a company that includes (from left) David Ahdar of the Chicago Civic Opera, Ualya Valentinoff of the Ballet Russe, Patricia Bowman of the Fokine Ballet, Alexis Rotov of the Mordkin Ballet and Orest of the Fokine Ballet.

>>> **1919** • Henry Kiel, the mayor of St. Louis, plays King Richard in "Robin Hood." Kiel helped to establish the outdoor theater in Forest Park, convinced that big, public productions can make a valuable contribution to civic life.

<<< 1940 • Brothers Jay and Lou Seiler have a specialty act that fits nicely into a Muny production of "Babes in Arms."

>>> 1940 • In a rare experiment, a straight play opens at The Muny. Fredric March stars in "The American Way"; Dickie Van Patten and Elinor Pittis play his grandchildren.

<<< 1976 • Singers and dancers perform at The Muny in a "Russian Festival of Music and Dance." The show — which features the Georgian State Dance Company, the Ukranian Dance Company, the Mengo Dance Ensemble and the Tadzhik Republic Performers — belongs to a long tradition of folkloric entertainment on the Forest Park stage.

>>> 2006 • Dan Betzler and Mary Luebke interpret "Aida" in American Sign Language for hearing-impaired theater-goers. Monday night has been ASL night at Muny shows since 1991. Described performances are also available on headsets for visually-impaired theater-goers.

1961 • The Muny works the St. Louis Hawks, a professional basketball team, into its production of "Wish You Were Here."

<<< 1955 • Early on a hazy Easter morning, the Rev. Dr. Wesley Hager of Grace Methodist Church delivers the sermon at a sunrise service at The Muny. The service, a tradition dating to 1926, is sponsored by the Metropolitan Church Federation.

THE WEATHER

An outdoor theater is at the mercy of the elements, and The Muny is the biggest outdoor theater of them all.

Through the years, however, the weather usually has been The Muny's friend. The theater sits in a natural depression in Forest Park, a place where heat can rise.

But except for the hottest, most humid nights, The Muny remains pleasant during the summer. The treasured breezes still blow, and the trees continue to shelter theater-goers from the worst of St. Louis' summer weather.

True, there still are nights when the performers take their curtain-calls in three-digit temperatures — nights when the sight of an actor dressed for winter in Russia evokes pure terror in audience members who know that it's really summer in St. Louis.

On those occasions, veteran Muny theater-goers wave their Chinese fans and relax. They sip another soda; they wait until it's just a few hours later, and the thermometer has dropped a little bit.

Mostly, they think that although it's great to have air-conditioning during the sun-kissed daylight hours, on a summer night all anybody really needs is a break, and a breeze, and a show.

>>> **1954** • Here's an idea: beat The Muny heat by pouring a thin film of water over the concrete slabs under the seats. This doesn't work as well as everyone hopes because the combination of water and St. Louis summers can make things steamy. Still, while the water runs, the performers enjoy it. Lunch hour brings a break from the heat to singers Barbara Craven (top), Sara Smith (seated below Craven), Kaye Geith (left, second row), Harlene Pomroy (right, second row) and Carolyn Hill (first row).

1946 • Rain is the curse of outdoor theater. Lucky patrons have umbrellas; others make do with jackets, newspapers and programs, or else crowd under the sheltered walkways that surround the theater. But few people leave; they know that the show will go on if at all possible. Since 1919, The Muny has averaged only 1.5 rainouts a year.

1937 • Some Muny supporters invite members of the chorus to parties at private pools year after year. It's a welcome relief and a chance to clown around.

1937 • Richard Berger, production manager of The Muny, and Evelyn Moser, a performer, sunbathe at a pool party for entertainers.

1948 • Singer Richard Kaeser and dancer Paula Skerik cool off after a show with slices of watermelon.

<<< 1938 • People who go to The Muny dress for the weather; performers don't have that choice. Children's chorus members (from left) Jean Knobbe, her twin sister Joan Knobbe, Clare Connelly and Jacqueline Stemmler bundle up in head-to-toe costumes for "The Gingerbread Man" – an August production!

>>> 1958 • In the days before air conditioning, The Muny cooled off its stars with rides in an official car, an Edsel convertible. As singers Janet Schaab, Pat Tucker, Mary Ann Heitzig and Cheri Ann Schear get ready to roll, Edsel manager Frank Corcoran hands Muny general manager Paul Beisman the keys to four cars.

EDSELS- Official Car
of the Municipal Opera
40th Anniversary Season
Courtesy
EDSEL DEALERS of St. Louis

1947 • Chorus girls welcome refreshing sodas as they rehearse for "Dancing Years."

>>> 1945 • In a rare quirk of St. Louis summer, members of The Muny's singing chorus try to stay warm during a cold snap.

>>> 1973 • Debbie Reynolds, who starred in the movie "Singin' in the Rain," finds herself in a similar position when a storm stops The Muny's production of "Irene." A trouper, Reynolds launches into a musical medley – starting with "Singin' in the Rain," of course – to entertain the audience until the show can resume.

THE CROWD

On a bad night at The Muny, maybe 6,000 people are in the seats.

A bad night at The Muny tops a stupendous night nearly anyplace else.

On a good night, the house count can swell to 10,000 theater-goers. Several times each summer, The Muny will sell out completely. That's 10,779 people. Before the seats were replaced and reconfigured in 2001, it was over 11,000.

Intimate theater this is not.

It is the opposite: The Muny is the largest outdoor theater in America.

It was built to give good entertainment to a whole community, not the culturally elite. It's art welded to democracy, an imaginative notion of civic life that finds real value in large numbers of people coming together to share music, ice cream and a summer breeze.

Granted, not all of them have a great view. But opera glasses, a big help, are available to rent, and many veteran patrons bring their own. The productions are designed to scale, with bright costumes, plenty of big dance numbers that make a beautiful panorama and extra-large sets.

At the beginning, Muny tickets cost 25 cents. Of course, that didn't last. A seat in the front of Terrace B cost 50 cents in 1925, $1 in 1955, $13 in 1985. By 2007, that seat cost $27.

If you buy a season ticket so you can sit in that seat for all seven shows, it's $154. Season tickets in the most expensive section, the box seats, are $441, but it's next to impossible to buy one. Box seats stay in families for generations.

The Muny's most venerated seats, however, still cost what they did when the theater opened: They're free. In the free seats at the top of the amphitheater, 1,456 people enjoy musicals every night all season. They need to get there early: It's first-come, first-served, and seats go fast.

The shows sound just as good as they do in down in the boxes, too.

Parking, along park streets or in the lots, is also free. Bring a picnic to enjoy in the park before the show where there's free entertainment every night, and The Muny remains a family-friendly bargain.

1948 • At 7 p.m., gates are unlocked, admitting happy theater-goers to The Muny.

2006 • Christine Diekman and David Hildebrand dance on the plaza at the top of The Muny, behind the free seats. There's often music for theater-goers before the start of a performance — in this case, before "The King and I."

1946 • All 1,700 free seats are filled, with an hour to go until showtime.

1922 • 8,000 people turn out for "The Queen's Lace Handkerchief" — not a record-breaking crowd but a good one. Look closely, and you'll spot many ushers in white caps and jackets.

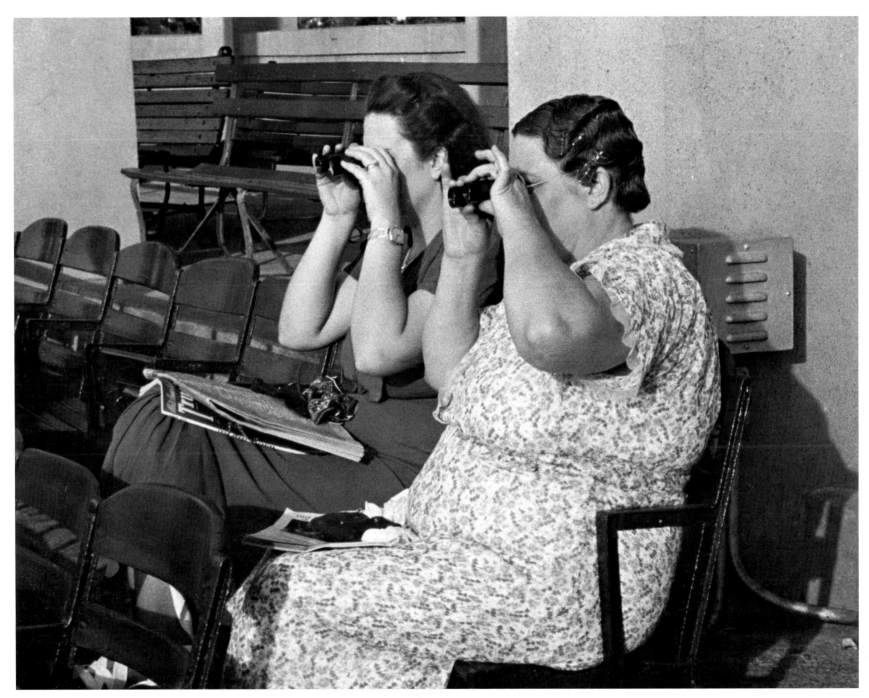

1938 • Many Muny-goers consider binoculars a big help, especially past the first section.

1941 • Singers and dancers at The Muny chat with soldiers from Jefferson Barracks who have come to see the show. Seated (from left) are Leonard Cannizaro, "Too Many Girls" star Joan Edwards, Alex Arunski, Betty Bruce and Honey Jean Waggoner. Frances Brenner, Thomas Woodruff and Maryon Dale stand behind them.

<<< 1948 • Cardinals Family Night brings out players' wives and children for a performance of "Hit the Deck." In the front row are (from left) Mickey Medwick, Mrs. Joe Medwick, Susie Medwick, Mrs. George Munger, Carolyn Munger, Diana Wilks, Mrs. Ted Wilks, Richard Musial and Mrs. Stan Musial. Behind them sit more Cardinal wives: (from left) Mrs. Murry Dickson, Mrs. Nippy Jones, Mrs. Terry Moore, Mrs. Harry Brecheen, Mrs. Don Lang and Mrs. Ralph LaPointe.

>>> 1977 • Fans line up to buy tickets at the start of the season. The shows include "Hello, Dolly!" with Carol Channing, "Wonderful Town" with Lauren Bacall, "The Sound of Music" with Shirley Jones and "Guys and Dolls" with Richard Roundtree and Leslie Uggams.

<<< 1957 • Joseph G. Toth, the 25 millionth person to pass through The Muny gates, his wife and their sons Bobby (left) and Joey say hello to the Tin Man (actor Harrison Muller). To mark the big number, The Muny gives the Toths passes to the 1958 season.

>>> 1956 • Members of the Frisco Railway Men's Club and their wives enjoy a box supper after a backstage tour and before they see "The Chocolate Soldier."

<<< 2001 • It's not unusual to see children in The Muny audience costumed like the characters onstage. Kathy Rose's daughters are ready for "The Wizard of Oz," with Taylor dressed as the Wicked Witch and Madison dressed as Dorothy. Their older sister, Nicole, is actually in the show, playing a Munchkin.

>>> 2000 • Many families enjoy a pre-show picnic in the park, especially on The Muny's unofficial picnic ground, the east side of the theater. Rosemary Neidel (center) and her friend Marjie Mader kick off the season with an opening-night birthday party.

THE SHOWS

What would today's audience make of The Muny's first seasons?

And what would those first Muny-goers think of shows like "Gypsy," "La Cage aux Folles" and "Grease"?

The early fashion for operettas, occasional operas and breezy revues took a sharp turn in 1927, when "Show Boat," by Jerome Kern and Oscar Hammerstein II, made its Broadway debut. With musical numbers that advanced the story and developed characters, "Show Boat" fundamentally changed musical theater. Naturally, that meant changes for The Muny — where "Show Boat" debuted just three years after its Broadway premiere.

Book musicals took the spotlight, introducing Muny-goers to many of the most important theater artists of the mid-20th century: Kern, Hammerstein, Richard Rodgers, Irving Berlin, George and Ira Gershwin, Cole Porter, Frank Loesser, Alan Jay Lerner and Frederick Loewe — the composers and lyricists who made Broadway, Broadway.

In 1957, "West Side Story" opened new directions for musical theater — more serious, less (far less!) comedic and very, very youthful. These impulses, too, would flourish at The Muny but so would their opposite, splashy shows like "Hello, Dolly!" and "Mame" that deliberately showcase more mature stars. There's room for both.

1926 • "Woodland" takes advantage of the young theater's outdoor setting with its title and its costumes. Note the chorus girls' hats, shaped like the heads of birds.

As the 20th century drew to a close, musical theater took on international dimensions. Big shows like "Cats," "Miss Saigon and "Les Misérables" from British and French artists — often without any spoken dialogue — came to dominate Broadway and London's West End. These, too, seemed suited to The Muny stage, where they could swell untrammeled to their natural proportions.

In the 2000s, The Muny has had a lot of luck with Broadway extravaganzas from Disney. It's a natural fit: family entertainment on a very, very big scale. Maybe Disney was taking notes.

<<< 1931 • "Nina Rosa," so popular that it plays The Muny six times between 1930 and 1950, typifies shows of its era: an exotic setting someplace south of the border, lots of Sigmund Romberg tunes, a plot that makes almost no sense. Though this scene might suggest otherwise, it's also a comedy. This production stars Guy Robertson (center) as the hero, Leonard Ceeley as the hot-tempered villain, and Gladys Baxter as Nina Rosa herself. Ceeley, Baxter and Robertson were favorites with Muny audiences, returning year after year.

2003 • Conner Gallagher appears in The Muny production of "Fiddler on the Roof."

>>> 2001 • Big dances full of folkloric costumes and swirling skirts are a Muny tradition. This Scottish number is featured in "Brigadoon."

1939 • Operettas served up like Viennese pastries, with loads of theatrical whipped cream, dominate The Muny's early years. Shows like "Waltz Dream" — starring Gladys Baxter (left), William Lynn (center) and Charles Kent — tended to involve lush music and silly hats in more or less equal proportions.

1945 • Chic modern touches - metallic shine, sleek lines - begin to influence the production style of numbers like "Begin the Beguine" in "Jubilee."

1958 • "Show Boat" is often considered the first real musical because it integrates musical numbers into the plot. It's also the most often-produced show in Muny history, with 14 productions so far.

>>> 1967 • Playing Anita and Bernardo, Carolyn Morris and Carmine Terra dance a mambo in "West Side Story" — the enormous hit by Leonard Bernstein and Stephen Sondheim based on "Romeo and Juliet." The show, which went a long way to showing that musicals need not be comedies, is among the productions that brought a new sophistication to The Muny season.

1966 • Eddie Albert stars in "The Music Man," a big show that might need to be cut down for a lot of theaters but not The Muny, which makes lavish productions of shows with period costumes a specialty.

1961 • Nearly every show at The Muny is family entertainment, but tradition demands a special children's show each season – such as Rodgers and Hammerstein's "Cinderella." Marie Santell plays the title role (center), with Harry Snow (kneeling, right) as Prince Charming and Mary Margaret Cook and Jack Gilford as his parents, the Queen and the King. Comics Hal LeRoy (left) and Will Able, dressed to the nines, play the ugly stepsisters.

<<< 1997 • From the mid-1980s on, Andrew Lloyd Webber's biblically inspired shows consistently drew huge Muny crowds. Jeb Brown rocks as the Elvis-like Pharaoh in "Joseph and the Amazing Technicolor Dreamcoat" (left), and Eric Kunze plays the title role in the 2005 production of "Jesus Christ Superstar" (above).

<<< **1996** • Lara Teeter stars in "Singin' in the Rain,"

1976 • Yul Brynner stars in his signature role, the king of Siam, in "The King and I," one of the Rodgers and Hammerstein Golden-Age musicals that epitomized The Muny style for decades.

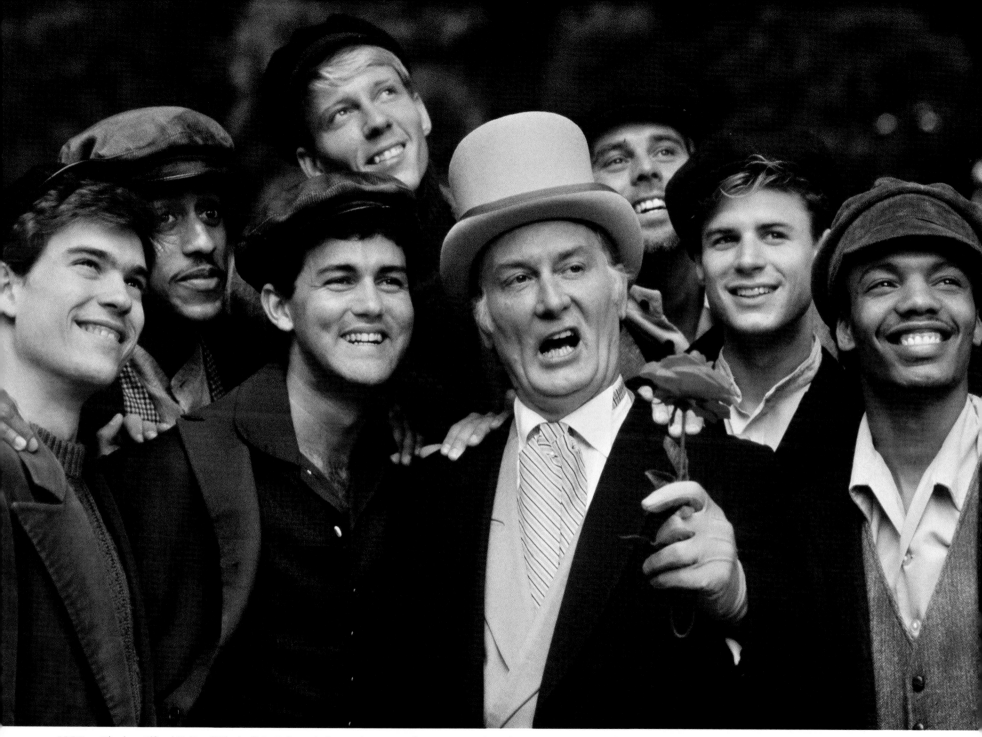

1985 • Playing Alfred P. Doolittle in "My Fair Lady," popular St. Louis actor Joneal Joplin (center) reminds friends to "get me to the church on time."

2001 • Judy McLane and Raymond Jaramillo McLeod star as Eva and Juan Peron in "Evita." The Muny, which usually mounts shows for only seven nights, discovered an eager audience for the mega-musicals that run for years at a stretch in London and New York.

<<< 1968 • Ecstatic dancing waiters greet Pearl Bailey in the big production number back from "Hello, Dolly!" Bailey stars opposite Cab Calloway.

2006 • Simone, daughter of the famed jazz singer Nina Simone, rehearses for "Aida" with the chorus. She plays the title role in the show by Sir Elton John, a musical that brought a rock-inflected sensibility to the outdoor theater.

<<< **2005** • Sarah Litzsinger, as Belle, struggles to break free of the horned and hirsute James Clow in "Beauty and the Beast," one of the Disney hits on Broadway that turned out to be a real winner with Muny-goers.

PHOTO CREDITS

FRONT COVER • 1933 • The Muny dance chorus rehearses at the outdoor theater in Forest Park.
THIS PAGE • 1939 • Without the pre-show crowd jostling for tickets, The Muny's elegant box office looks serene late at night.
BACK COVER • 2006 • Dirk Lumbard and Shannon M. O'Bryan dance a duet in Irving Berlin's "White Christmas," a show created for the stage by Muny executive producer Paul Blake.